I can't keep calm I'm Indian! - A quick guide to learn CALM for a stress-free living

by

ATHARVA INAMDAR

TABLE OF CONTENTS

Section	Page
Introduction	1
CHAPTER ONE - The Uninvited Guest: Understanding This Daily Tension	3
CHAPTER TWO - Your Body's Alarm System: How Stress Affects Your Health	5
CHAPTER THREE - The Gift of Calm: Finding Your Body's Off-Switch	8
CHAPTER FOUR - The Unbreakable Spirit: The Courage to Get Back Up	13
CHAPTER FIVE - Simple Tools for a Calmer You	17
CHAPTER SIX - The Art of Being Your Own Best Friend	21
CHAPTER SEVEN - Weaving Peace into Your Busy Day: Simple Daily Habits	26
CHAPTER EIGHT - Finding Your Own Path: Creating a Plan for Your Life	30
CHAPTER NINE - "But I Have No Time..." and Other Truths About Stress	34
CHAPTER TEN - Finding Your 'Why': The Path to Lasting Peace	37

INTRODUCTION

Let me ask you something. When was the last time you felt truly, deeply relaxed? A moment with no worry, no to-do list running in your mind, just quiet, peaceful calm?

If you can't remember, you're not alone. Believe me. It seems that for most of us—a staggering 80% of adults—stress has become a daily companion. We're all running a race we never signed up for, and the finish line keeps moving further away.

But this is more than just a feeling of being tired or busy. This constant tension is a silent thief. It steals our joy, our peace, and slowly, it begins to steal our health. It quietly increases our risk of the very illnesses we fear most: heart disease, diabetes, and even cancer. It affects our mental well-being, creating a shadow of anxiety and sadness that we often feel we have to hide from the world.

My name is Atharva Inamdar, and I have spent my life telling stories. After writing more than 1500 books, I've learned that the most important story is the one we tell ourselves about our own lives. And I have seen, time and again, how unspoken stress can write a very unhappy ending.

My first lessons in strength didn't come from a book, but from living with my family in Pune. It's there I first saw how our thoughts could make us sick, and how a mother's loving touch could soothe a fever. I saw the mind-body connection in action every single day.

And that's why I'm writing this book, for you. I want to share simple, powerful truths that blend our ancient Indian wisdom with modern science. Whether you're a student in Kota facing the pressure of exams, an IT professional in Bangalore working late nights, or a homemaker in Bhilai managing a thousand different duties, this book is for you. Think of me as your companion on this journey.

The tools I will share are life-changing. I have seen it with my own eyes. I want to bring these years of learning directly to you. Stress will always be there, yes, but it does not have to be the director of your life's story.

We will explore some science, but I promise it won't be like a boring school lecture. I'll share it through stories, simple examples, and maybe even a little humour. We will rediscover a truth our ancestors knew well: **our mind is the master of our body.**

CHAPTER ONE - The Uninvited Guest: Understanding This Daily *Tension*

Have you been stuck at a traffic jam? Say at the Silk Board junction in Bangalore? The noise of the horns, the heat, the feeling of being completely trapped and powerless. You want to move forward, but you can't. That chaos? That frustration? That is exactly what stress does to our mind.

In today's world, stress is like that uninvited relative who shows up without warning, eats all the snacks, and creates a mess before leaving. It comes from everywhere—a tough deadline at work, a family argument, a child's exams, or even just the constant *ping* of your WhatsApp. But what is it, really? To win a battle, you must first know your enemy. So let's understand what stress is, and why it has such a powerful hold on us.

The Biology of Stress: What's Happening Inside Your Body

Think of your body as a country. Your brain is the government. It has an ancient, very effective alarm system. When this government perceives a threat—it could be a real threat like a snake on the path, or a perceived threat like the fear of public speaking—it pushes a big red button.

This button activates the **stress response**. It's a survival mechanism, a gift from our ancestors to help them fight or run away from a tiger. The problem is, our brains today can't tell the difference between a tiger and an angry email from our boss. It pushes the same red button.

When the button is pushed, a special commander is released into your body. This commander's name is **Cortisol**. It's your main stress hormone. Cortisol's job is to prepare the country for emergency. It quickly raises the sugar in your blood for instant energy. It increases your heart rate and blood pressure. It makes you hyper-alert. It also smartly shuts down non-essential services, like your digestive system. After all, you don't need to digest lunch when you're running from a tiger!

This is your **"fight-or-flight"** response. It's brilliant for short, intense dangers. But what happens when the alarm is ringing all day, every day?

That's when we get **chronic stress**. And chronic stress leads to **burnout**. Burnout isn't just feeling tired. It's a bone-deep weariness. It's when you feel emotionally, mentally, and physically empty, like a phone battery that is stuck at 1%.

All this chronic stress creates something called **allostatic load**.

But when you start to understand that stress isn't just a feeling in your head but a powerful physical process, you can start to take back control.

Stress in the Modern Indian World: Our Unique Pressures

You've just settled down with a hot cup of tea, looking forward to a few moments of peace. And then it begins. The phone buzzes. A family WhatsApp group is debating something. An old school friend has posted pictures of their perfect European holiday. Your email reminds you of the presentation you haven't finished.

Our phones have connected us to the world, but they have disconnected us from ourselves. We live in a world of constant comparison. We scroll through Instagram and feel our lives are not good enough. We see others' successes and feel like we are falling behind. This creates a terrible pressure to be perfect, to always be achieving, to never show weakness.

And then there are the pressures we Indians know so well. The silent weight of expectations. The pressure to get the right job, to earn a certain amount, to get married by a certain age, to make sure your children are ahead in their class, to take care of ageing parents, to keep all the relatives happy. It's an endless list.

We run this race every day, and in the process, we sacrifice the most important things: our sleep, our peace of mind, and our health. We stay up late, scrolling on our phones, the blue light telling our brains it's still daytime. We wake up exhausted and reach for more and more caffeine just to function. It becomes a cycle, a trap.

But here's the good news: you hold the key to this trap. You can choose to set boundaries. You can decide that mealtimes are for family, not for phones. You can create a simple rule to switch off all screens an hour before you sleep. You can consciously take a few minutes to just sit in your balcony, listen to the birds, and unplug from the digital noise.

By taking these small steps, you are not just managing your time. You are reclaiming your life.

CHAPTER TWO - Your Body's Alarm System: How Stress Affects Your Health

I recall a time when I was riding in an auto-rickshaw heading towards the airport The driver was skilfully weaving through traffic, almost like a movie hero. Suddenly, a bus came right in front of us, and my driver slammed on the brakes. For one long second, everything went silent. It felt as though my heart had stopped. Then, just as quickly, it started pounding like a drum. My hands were gripping the metal bar so tightly my knuckles were white.

What I felt in that moment was the **innate stress response**. It's the purest, most ancient survival instinct we have. It's automatic. It's powerful. And it's inside every single one of us.

When my brain saw that bus, it didn't stop to think. It just acted. It flooded my body with adrenalin. It prepared my muscles to either brace for impact (fight) or somehow jump out of the way (flight). All this happened in less than a second. It's a beautiful, life-saving system.

But here's the problem. This same powerful system can be triggered when your son brings home a bad report card, or when you have a disagreement with your spouse. The body doesn't know the difference. It reacts with the same intensity, preparing for a life-or-death battle that isn't actually there. When this happens day after day, our life-saving system starts to cause us harm.

The Role of Cortisol: A Guest Who Overstays

Let's talk more about Cortisol, our body's stress commander. Think of cortisol like a special guest who arrives for a big family wedding. For those few days, they are incredibly helpful. They manage things, organize people, and make sure everything runs smoothly. You are grateful they are there. That's cortisol during short-term stress—a friend.

But what if the wedding is over, and the guest refuses to leave? They stay for weeks, then months. They start telling you how to run your house. They eat all your food. They create tension. The helpful guest has now become a major problem. That's cortisol during long-term, chronic stress—a foe.

When cortisol stays high for too long, it starts to damage the house, which is your body. It weakens your immune system, making it easier for you to get sick. It messes with your sleep. It increases your appetite for unhealthy, sugary foods and tells your body to store fat, especially around your belly. So, cortisol isn't bad. Too much cortisol, for too long, is the real problem.

Chronic Stress and Disease: The Silent Connection

In India today, we are facing an epidemic of lifestyle diseases like heart attacks and diabetes. We often blame our food or lack of exercise. But we ignore one of the biggest culprits: chronic stress. Let me be very clear: the connection between long-term stress and serious illness is not a theory. It is a scientific fact.

- **Your Heart:** Constant stress is like putting your heart under pressure all day long. It leads to high blood pressure, which is a silent killer. Over time, it damages your arteries and dramatically increases your risk of a heart attack.
- **Diabetes:** Stress plays havoc with your blood sugar. High cortisol levels make it difficult for your body to manage sugar properly, which can lead to type 2 diabetes.
- **Your Immunity:** Your immune system is your personal army against germs. Stress is like a corrupt general who weakens this army from the inside. When your immunity is low, you become vulnerable to every infection, from a common cold to more serious illnesses.
- **Inflammation:** Stress creates a slow, invisible fire inside your body called inflammation. Scientists now believe that this chronic inflammation is a root cause of many major diseases.

Understanding this connection is incredibly empowering. It means that by learning to manage your stress, you are not just improving your mood. You are actively protecting yourself from some of the most dangerous diseases of our time.

Brain on Stress: When Thinking Becomes Difficult

Stress behaves like a very persistent telemarketer for your brain. It keeps calling, distracting you, and filling your head with worries. It directly impacts how your brain functions. The emotional, fearful part of your brain (the amygdala) becomes loud and overactive. The calm, logical, decision-making part of your brain (the prefrontal cortex) becomes quiet and weak.

This imbalance affects you in very real ways:

- **Memory Fog:** You start forgetting things—names, appointments, why you walked into a room.
- **Lost Focus:** You find it hard to concentrate. Your mind feels scattered, jumping from one thought to the next.
- **Difficult Decisions:** Even small choices feel overwhelming.
- **Emotional Rollercoaster:** You may feel anxious for no reason, become easily irritated, or feel a persistent sadness that you can't shake off.

It's not your fault. It's your brain on stress.

Emotional Burnout: The Empty Well

Imagine a well from which a whole village gets its water. Every day, people draw water, but no one thinks about filling it back up. One day, someone lowers a bucket and it comes up empty. The well has run dry.

That empty well is **emotional burnout**. It's what happens when you keep giving and giving—at work, to your family, to your responsibilities—without taking time to refill your own emotional and mental reserves. It's more than just tiredness. It's a deep emptiness.

Let me tell you about Ananya, a brilliant software engineer from Bangalore. She was living the dream—good job, good salary, making her parents proud. She worked 12-hour days, handled clients from America, and never said no to extra work. She was also dealing with the constant family pressure to "settle down." She ignored the signs—the acidity, the headaches, the feeling of dread on Sunday nights. "This is the price of success," she told herself.

The final straw wasn't some big disaster. It was a simple question from her mother one evening: "What would you like for dinner?" Ananya just burst into tears. She had nothing left. No energy to even make a simple choice. She had hit burnout.

Ananya's story has a hopeful ending. She sought help. She learned to set boundaries. She started saying "no." She rediscovered her old love for painting, an activity that filled her well back up. Her story is a powerful reminder: you cannot pour from an empty cup. Self-care isn't selfish; it's essential for survival.

The Gut-Brain Axis: Your Stomach is Your Second Brain

For thousands of years in India, our elders and teachers have told us this: a healthy life begins with a healthy stomach. They knew that the state of our digestion affects our mood, our energy, and our thoughts.

Modern science has finally caught up with this ancient wisdom. They call it the **gut-brain axis**. Simply put, there is a superhighway of communication between your gut and your brain. They are constantly sending messages back and forth.

When you feel stressed or anxious, your brain sends distress signals to your gut. This is why you get that "butterflies in your stomach" feeling, or suffer from acidity, gas, or an upset stomach during tense times. But it works the other way too. An unhealthy gut can send signals to the brain that increase feelings of anxiety and stress.

The heroes of this story are the trillions of good bacteria living in your gut. They are like a vast, friendly army that helps keep you healthy and resilient. You can support this army by eating the right foods. That simple bowl of *dahi* your mother tells you to eat? She's right. It's full of **probiotics**—the good bacteria. Eating foods with plenty of fibre (**prebiotics**) gives this army the food it needs to thrive.

So, when you take care of your gut, you are taking direct care of your brain. Stress isn't just in your head. It's a full-body experience. And the path to a calmer mind often begins in your stomach. In the chapters to come, we will explore many more simple, powerful ways to manage this system and build a healthier, happier life.

CHAPTER THREE - The Gift of Calm: Finding Your Body's Off-Switch

Here is the good news. There is hope.

Think of your body like a pressure cooker on the stove. The daily pressures of work, family, and a never-ending to-do list keep turning up the heat. The pressure builds and builds. You can hear the whistle start to hiss. You feel like you are about to explode.

Just when you think you can't take any more, you reach out and gently turn off the flame. You hear a soft release of steam. The pressure goes down. The whistle becomes quiet. Your kitchen is calm again.

This gentle release is what we call the **"relaxation response."** It is your body's natural, built-in "off-switch" for stress. It is our biological reset button. A brilliant doctor, Dr. Herbert Benson, first gave this process a name. He showed us that just as our body has a system to get worked up (the fight-or-flight response), it also has a system to calm down.

This calming system is called the **parasympathetic nervous system**. You can think of it as the "rest and digest" part of your government. When it takes charge, magic happens. It's like switching from a strong, sugary cup of cutting *chai* that makes you feel wired, to a warm, soothing cup of *tulsi* tea. Your heart rate slows down, your blood pressure lowers, and the tight knots in your muscles begin to loosen.

The relaxation response is your body's way of saying, *"Chalo, it's time to rest now."* It pushes back against the frenzy of fight-or-flight. Your heart, which was beating like a drum at a festival, finally calms down. Your blood pressure takes a much-needed holiday. Your body gets a chance to repair and recharge. This is not just about feeling good for a moment. It is about building a foundation of health and strength that lasts a lifetime.

So, how do you flip this magical switch? You don't need to be a yogi sitting on a mountain top. The relaxation response is available to every single one of us. It is our birthright. Simple practices, like focusing on your breath or repeating a calming word in your mind, can invite this peace to enter. The beauty of these techniques is their simplicity. They can fit into the busiest of lives, in the middle of the most chaotic days.

When you learn to use this switch, the effect on your life is profound. It's like finding a cool, shady spot on a hot summer afternoon. You become better at handling life's problems with a calm mind. You learn to respond to situations, instead of just reacting to them. And as your stress levels go down, your immune system gets stronger. That means fewer sick days and more energy for the things you love. It's the most natural, side-effect-free medicine in the world.

A Moment for You: Reflection Exercise

Take a moment right now. Close your eyes if you feel comfortable. Think of a time when you felt truly, deeply relaxed and peaceful. Where were you? Maybe it was sitting in your balcony during a quiet morning, listening to the birds. Perhaps it was a walk in a park, or a moment of laughter with your family. What did it feel like in your body? Try to bring that feeling back. Think about how you can bring more of those simple, peaceful moments into your life, starting today.

Embracing the relaxation response is not just about managing stress. It's about taking back your life from the grip of constant *tension*. It is about creating a small temple of calm inside yourself, a place you can go to no matter what is happening on the outside.

Breathing: The Master Key in Your Pocket

Imagine you are in the middle of a hectic day. Your phone is ringing, your boss wants a report, and you have a hundred things to do. Your mind feels like a tangled ball of wool.

Now, imagine you have a master key in your pocket. A key that can unlock a door to a quiet, peaceful room, right in the middle of all that chaos.

That master key is your breath.

For thousands of years in India, our yogis and sages have taught us the power of *Pranayama*—the art of controlling the breath. They knew that breathing isn't just something our body does on its own. It is a powerful tool we can use to control our mind and our stress.

When you take slow, deep breaths that fill your belly, you are sending a powerful signal to your brain. You are telling it: "Everything is okay. It is safe to relax now." This simple act activates your "rest and digest" system. Your heart rate slows, your blood pressure drops, and the level of the stress hormone, cortisol, goes down.

There are many simple breathing techniques. Let me share two of my favourites.

1. **Belly Breathing:** This is the most basic and powerful technique. Sit or lie down comfortably. Place one hand on your chest and the other on your belly. As you breathe in slowly through your nose, imagine your belly is a balloon. Let it fill with air and expand. Your hand on your belly should rise. As you breathe out slowly, let the balloon deflate. Your hand should go down. Try to keep the hand on your chest still. This ensures you are breathing deeply.
2. **Box Breathing:** This is a simple counting technique used by everyone from soldiers to students to stay calm under pressure. It's very easy. Breathe in for a count of four. Hold your breath for a count of four. Breathe out for a count of four. Hold your breath again for a count of four. That's one "box." Repeat this a few times. It brings instant focus and calm.

To get the most benefit, try to practice for just a few minutes every day. Consistency is the key.

Let me tell you about Samruddhi, a young college student in Nashik. The pressure of her final exams was immense. She would study all night, her mind racing with anxiety. She felt like she couldn't breathe. Her father taught her the simple belly breathing technique. Whenever she felt the panic rising, she would find a quiet corner, close her eyes, and just breathe. In for four counts, out for six. It became her secret weapon, her anchor in the stormy sea of exams. It didn't make the exams disappear, but it gave her the calm and focus to face them.

Your breath is always with you. It costs nothing. It takes only a few minutes. Next time you feel overwhelmed, remember this master key in your pocket. Unlock the door to your inner peace.

Mind-Body Medicine: A Two-Way Street

Have you ever felt your mouth go dry just before you have to give a presentation? Or felt your stomach churn with nerves before an important meeting? That is the mind-body connection in action.

Think of your mind and body as being connected by a busy, two-way street. What happens in your mind directly affects your body. And what happens in your body directly affects your mind. They are in a constant conversation.

When your mind is full of worry and stress, your body listens. It can react with real, physical symptoms. This is where we get headaches, acidity, back pain, and so many other issues that doctors call "psychosomatic." This doesn’t mean the pain is "all in your head." The pain is very real. It simply means the root cause of the physical problem might be emotional or mental stress.

Let me tell you about a friend of mine, Dr. Pathania. Shee is a senior doctor in a large, busy government hospital in Dehradoon. She is a wonderful woman, dedicated to her patients. But the stress of her job was enormous. Every day was a crisis. She started getting terrible migraine headaches. They would come like clockwork during her busiest weeks. She took painkillers, but they only helped a little.

Finally, she realized the connection. Her stress was triggering the migraines. The worry in her mind was creating real pain in her head. She started using the mind-body tools in this book. She began a simple 10-minute breathing practice every morning. She learned to notice her stress signals and take short breaks during the day. Slowly but surely, the frequency and intensity of her migraines reduced dramatically.

Your mind is incredibly powerful. Just as it can create illness, it can also create health. Mindfulness is a powerful tool here. It is the practice of paying attention to the present moment without judgment. When you are mindful, you create a small space of calm within you. Studies have shown that mindfulness can lower blood pressure, improve your immune system, and reduce stress. It’s like your mind and body finally sign a peace treaty and agree to work together.

Recognizing this two-way street is the first step. It empowers you to look beyond just the physical symptoms. It helps you understand that to heal your body, you must also soothe your mind.

Emotions and How Your Body Responds

Imagine you are walking home late one night down a dark, empty street. Suddenly, you hear footsteps behind you. Your heart starts pounding. Your muscles become tight. You start walking faster. That intense feeling is fear. It is your body's "fight-or-flight" response, preparing you for danger.

Our emotions are not just feelings. They are powerful physical events. Each emotion sends a different set of chemical messages throughout your body.

When you feel love, safety, or joy, your body responds with the relaxation response. Your heart rate slows down, your muscles relax. This is a state of healing and repair.

But difficult emotions, when they last for a long time, can be harmful. Chronic anger is like a slow poison. It can keep your blood pressure high, putting you at risk for heart problems. Long-term sadness can weaken your immune system, making you more likely to fall sick.

This is why **emotional awareness** is so important. It is the ability to notice and understand what you are feeling, without letting the feeling take over. It’s not about stopping your emotions. It's about becoming the calm observer of your own inner world.

Think of yourself as the conductor of an orchestra. Your emotions are the different instruments. Sometimes the drums of anger are loud, sometimes the violins of sadness are playing. As the conductor, your job is not to silence any instrument, but to bring them all into harmony.

Imagine you are stuck in a terrible traffic jam. You feel the anger rising. Your fists are clenched, your jaw is tight. Now, instead of honking or shouting, just notice the feeling. Say to yourself, "Okay, I am feeling angry right now." Take a deep breath. Acknowledge the emotion without acting on it. This simple act of awareness can stop the emotion from hijacking your body's stress response. It gives you back your power.

Emotions are the colours of life. By understanding how they affect our bodies, we can learn to paint a masterpiece of health and well-being.

Your Thoughts and Your Physical Health

Have you ever noticed how the exact same situation can feel very different depending on your mood? This is the power of your thoughts.

Imagine your boss gives you a difficult project with a tight deadline.

- **Thought A:** *"Oh no, this is impossible! I am going to fail. My boss will be so angry."* How does your body feel? Tense, anxious, stressed.
- **Thought B:** *"Okay, this is a challenge. But it's an opportunity to show what I can do. I will break it down into small steps and get it done."* How does your body feel now? More energized, focused, and in control.

The situation is the same. Your thoughts about the situation are what changed your body's response. How you *see* things changes how you *feel* things.

A negative mindset, where you are always expecting the worst, acts like a black cloud that follows you around. This negativity has real physical effects. Constantly replaying negative thoughts in your mind (this is called rumination) can increase chronic pain and make you more likely to get sick.

But the opposite is also true. The power of positive belief is incredible. You have probably heard of the **placebo effect**. This is when a patient gets better after taking a sugar pill, simply because they *believe* it is real medicine. This is not magic. It is the mind's powerful ability to influence the body's healing process. An optimistic outlook can genuinely help you recover faster from illness.

So, how can we use this power? We can practice **changing the way we think**. This is like giving your mind a software update. When you catch a negative thought, you can learn to question it. Is it really 100% true? Is there another way to look at this situation?

Mindfulness is a great help here. Imagine you are sitting on the bank of a river. Your thoughts are like leaves floating by on the water. You don't have to jump into the river and grab every leaf. You can simply sit and watch them float by. This practice helps you realize that you are not your thoughts. You are the observer of your thoughts. This creates a space of peace.

As we finish this chapter, remember this: your mind is your greatest ally in the journey to a stress-free life. By learning to use the tools of relaxation, breathing, and mindful thinking, you can turn down the heat of stress and find the calm that is always waiting for you inside.

CHAPTER FOUR - The Unbreakable Spirit: The Courage to Get Back Up

Imagine life is like a game of gully cricket. The pitch is uneven, the rules change without warning, and the ball can come at you from any direction. Some days you hit a six, feeling like a champion. Other days, you get out on the first ball, or the ball hits you hard when you aren't looking.

The secret to this game isn't about never getting out. It's about how you walk back to the pitch after you've been hit. That is **resilience**. Resilience is our *himmat*, our inner strength. It is the ability to bounce back, to rise after every fall, and to keep playing the game of life, no matter how many times we get knocked down.

Resilience is like that one friend who always believes in you. The one who puts a hand on your shoulder and says, "Don't worry, you've got this!" when you feel like giving up. It is the mental toughness that helps us face setbacks—a job loss, a personal failure, a family crisis—and still keep our balance. People with resilience are not superhuman; they don't avoid pain or stress. But they have a special skill: they learn from every difficulty. They use their failures as stepping stones to climb higher.

For Smita, she learned about resilience not in a classroom, but in the courtyard of her joint family home. Life in that home taught her that you have to be tough and flexible at the same time. If she fell while playing, she was expected to get up, brush the dust off her clothes, and get back in the game. There was no time for endless sympathy. That was a tough lesson, but a valuable one. It taught her that life isn't always fair, but you always have the choice to keep moving forward.

Building resilience is like strengthening a muscle. The more you use it, the stronger it gets. In this book, we will explore simple, practical exercises to build this inner muscle. From practicing gratitude to setting small, achievable goals, these activities will prepare your mind and spirit to face any challenge with confidence.

Believe it or not, difficult times are the best teachers of resilience. When we face challenges, it's like life is sending us to a boot camp. Each problem is a test of our strength. It's in these moments of hardship that our resilience is truly born. Every failure is a chance to learn, to change our direction, and to grow. It's like when you are learning to cook and you burn the bhakari the first time. The next one will be better because you learned from your mistake.

Developing a **growth mindset** is the key. This is the belief that you can always learn and improve. It shifts your thinking from "I can't do this" to "I can't do this... *yet*." With this mindset, you see challenges not as threats, but as opportunities. This belief is like the wind in your sails, always pushing you forward.

And remember, resilience is not a solo journey. The great Indian epic, the Mahabharata, teaches us the importance of having allies. We need a support network—our family, our friends, our community. They are our safety net, there to catch us when we fall and to cheer us on. Even a hero like Arjun needed a guide like Krishna.

A Moment for You: Resilience Reflection

Take a moment to think about a difficult time in your life that you overcame. It could be big or small. What did you learn from that experience? How did it make you stronger? Write down your thoughts. This is not just a memory; it is proof of your own inner strength. Remind yourself of it often.

Years ago, during the most difficult phase of my life, I found myself sitting in a counsellor's office. My relationship was ending, and my heart was in pieces. My counsellor, a young woman named Yukti Khushu, gave me some advice that felt hard to hear at the time. She said, "Atharva, there is no shortcut through this pain. The only way is through it. Do the hard work of healing now, and one day, you will look back and see the strength you have built."

Honestly, I just wanted the pain to go away. But her words stayed with me. Slowly, I started to understand. Over the years, I stopped trying to run away from my feelings and instead, I faced them. It was the hardest thing I ever did, but it was also the greatest gift I ever gave myself. It's never too late, you can always start today and make the rest of your life better.

Seeing Stress as a Teacher

We usually think of stress as a bad thing, an enemy we have to fight. But what if we change our perspective? What if we start to see stress as a teacher, a rather strict one, but a teacher nonetheless?

When we see challenges as opportunities to grow, something magical happens. The stress doesn't disappear, but our relationship with it changes. This is not about pretending that stress feels good. It is about understanding that stepping out of our comfort zone is the only way we can grow.

Our brain is a magnificent organ. It has something called **plasticity**, which means it can change and adapt. Like a muscle, it gets stronger with exercise. When we face manageable stress, it's like a workout for our brain. It forces our brain to create new connections, making us better at solving problems and thinking creatively.

This is called **stress-related growth**. When you go through a stressful experience and come out on the other side, you are not the same person. You are stronger. You are wiser. Your problem-solving skills are sharper. Your **emotional intelligence**—your ability to understand your own emotions and those of others—also gets a big boost. You become a more mature and compassionate human being.

Think about the Indian cricket team that won the World Cup in 1983 *(no matter how boring I find that movie '83, my dad loves it.)* They were the underdogs, facing immense pressure. But they used that stress as fuel and created history.

I still remember my bike ride I took in the Himalayan Mountains, right in the middle of that difficult period in my life. A friend had invited me, and I went without much thought. The morning was beautiful, the sky was a perfect blue.

But as we climbed higher, the weather turned suddenly. Breathing became difficult. I had no proper jacket for the extreme cold, I was shivering and miserable. I remember thinking, "This is just like my life right now: cold, miserable, and completely joyless."

But an hour later, as we made our way down, the storm passed as quickly as it had come. The sun came out, and a beautiful rainbow appeared over the valley. In that moment, surrounded by such breathtaking beauty, I felt a deep sense of peace. It hit me then—this storm, too, shall pass. I realised that the storm inside my heart would also fade away one day, and the sun would shine again. Life always turns a corner, even when we can't see it.

Biofeedback: Listening to Your Body's Language

Imagine you are driving a car but there is no dashboard. You don't know your speed, you don't know how much petrol is left. It would be a very stressful drive, wouldn't it?

Living without being aware of your body's stress signals is like driving that car. **Biofeedback** is like installing a dashboard for your body. It is a technique that helps you listen to your body's signals. It shows you, in real-time, how your thoughts and feelings are affecting your body. For example, it can measure your heart rate, your muscle tension, or even the temperature of your skin.

When you see how your heart rate goes up during a tense meeting, you learn to recognise that signal. This awareness is the first step to control. Biofeedback teaches you to consciously change your body's response. You learn to slow your heart rate down with deep breathing. You learn to relax your muscles when they get tight.

It empowers you. It's like learning the language of your own body. Athletes use it to stay calm during high-pressure competitions. Cricketers uses it to manage themselves during tournaments. Why do you think Mahendra Singh Dhoni was able to be absolutely calm and ready for the final over blitz when others kinda flattered, because he used his awareness to notice his racing heart. He then takes a few deep breaths to calm himself, allowing him to play with focus and precision.

Biofeedback is not about complicated machines. It's about a simple, powerful idea: listen to your body. It is always talking to you. When you learn to listen, you can respond with care, and turn stress into strength.

Heart Rate Variability (HRV): The Rhythm of a Healthy Heart

Imagine your heart is a talented tabla player. A good tabla player doesn't play with a robotic, unchanging beat. They play with rhythm, with variation, with life.

Heart Rate Variability (HRV) is a measure of this healthy variation in your heartbeat. It might sound strange, but a heart that has more variability in its rhythm is actually a healthier, more resilient heart.

A high HRV is a sign that your body is very good at adapting to stress. It means your "rest and digest" system is working well. It's like having a good suspension system in your car that can handle bumpy roads smoothly. A low HRV, on the other hand, can be a sign that your body is stuck in stress mode.

Today, many simple watches and fitness trackers can measure your HRV. It can be a very useful tool. It gives you a window into how well your body is coping with stress.

How can you improve your HRV?

- **Regular Exercise:** A simple morning walk or a game of badminton strengthens your heart's resilience.
- **Good Sleep:** Sleep is like a nightly service for your heart, allowing it to recover.
- **Stress Management:** Practices like meditation and deep breathing directly train your nervous system to be more balanced, which improves your HRV.
- **Healthy Food:** A balanced, home-cooked meal nourishes your body and supports its ability to handle stress.

Your HRV is more than just a number. It is a reflection of your body's inner strength. By taking care of your lifestyle, you are not just living a healthier life—you are composing a beautiful, resilient rhythm for your heart.

CHAPTER FIVE - Simple Tools for a Calmer You

Imagine your mind is like a busy marketplace, like Chandni Chowk in Delhi. There are thousands of thoughts, worries, and ideas all shouting for your attention at the same time. It's noisy, chaotic, and overwhelming.

Meditation, or *Dhyana* as our ancestors called it, is not about shutting down the entire market. That's impossible. It is simply about finding a quiet corner in that market, sitting down, and just breathing. It's about gently bringing your focus to one single point, like your breath, and giving your mind a much-needed rest from the chaos.

For thousands of years, our sages and rishis have known the power of meditation. Now, modern science is proving them right. Science shows that regular meditation can actually change your brain. It's like a workout for your brain cells. It can strengthen the parts of your brain responsible for memory, focus, and emotional control. It's like upgrading your brain's internal software, helping you run your life more smoothly and calmly.

The benefits are not just in the brain. Regular meditation can lower your blood pressure and heart rate. It switches off your body's "fight-or-flight" response. It's like turning down the volume on a loud, stressful song and playing a soft, soothing melody instead. It even boosts your immune system, your body's army against illness.

You don't need to take my word for it. Thousands of studies have shown that meditation is one of the most powerful tools for reducing stress, anxiety, and depression. It's like a natural, side-effect-free medicine for your mind.

A Moment for You: Meditation Exploration Exercise

Let's try a simple exercise right now. Find a quiet place to sit. You can sit on a chair or on the floor, whatever is comfortable. Close your eyes. Now, just bring your attention to your breath. Don't try to change it. Just notice the feeling of the air coming in through your nose, and going out. Your mind will wander. That's its job. You will think about your to-do list, your family, your worries. When you notice your mind has wandered, gently, without any judgment, bring your attention back to your breath. Do this again and again. Try it for just two minutes. That's it. You have just meditated.

Beginner's Guide to Mindfulness: Living in the Now

Imagine you are sitting at a busy railway station. Trains of thought are constantly arriving and departing. The train of the past, filled with memories and regrets. The train of the future, filled with worries and plans.

Mindfulness is the art of simply sitting on the platform and watching these trains come and go, without getting on any of them. It is the simple practice of being fully aware of the present moment, right here, right now, without judgment.

Mindfulness is a simple but profound idea. It is about paying attention. You can practice it anywhere, anytime. When you are drinking your morning *cup of tea* instead of scrolling through your phone, just drink the *god-damn tea!*. Feel the warmth of the cup. Taste the flavour of the ginger and cardamom. Notice the aroma. That is mindfulness.

When you are walking, feel your feet on the ground. Notice the world around you. The trees, the sky, the people. That is mindfulness.

Regular mindfulness practice is like cleaning the cluttered rooms of your mind. It sharpens your focus. It cales your anxiety. It teaches you to respond to life's challenges with calm wisdom, instead of reacting with panic.

Of course, it's not always easy. Your mind will wander. That's normal. The practice of mindfulness is not about having an empty mind. It is about gently bringing your mind back to the present moment, over and over again, with kindness and patience.

Progressive Muscle Relaxation: The Art of Letting Go

Imagine your body is a tightly clenched fist. All day long, because of stress, your muscles—in your shoulders, your neck, your jaw—are tight and tense. You may not even notice it.

Progressive Muscle Relaxation (PMR) is a simple and wonderful technique that teaches your body how to let go of this tension. It is very similar to the ancient yogic practice of **Yoga Nidra**.

The idea is simple. You systematically tense and then relax different muscle groups in your body, one by one. You start with your feet. You curl your toes tightly for a few seconds, feeling the tension. Then, you release them completely, feeling the wave of relaxation that follows. You do this with your legs, your stomach, your hands, your arms, your shoulders, and even your face.

This practice does two amazing things. First, it deeply relaxes your body. Second, it makes you more aware of where you hold tension. Over time, you can learn to release this tension even in the middle of a stressful day.

Regular practice of PMR can greatly improve your sleep. It can reduce stress-related aches and pains. You don't need any special equipment. Just a quiet place where you can lie down for 10-15 minutes and listen to your body. It is a beautiful gift of relaxation that you can give to yourself every day.

Visualization and Guided Imagery: The Cinema of Your Mind

Imagine you are sitting on a quiet beach on the coast of Goa. You can feel the warm sun on your skin. You can hear the gentle sound of the waves. You can feel the soft sea breeze.

You are not actually there. But in your mind, you can be. That is the power of **visualization** and **guided imagery**.

These techniques are like using your mind to create a personal cinema. You are the director, and you can create any peaceful scene you want. Visualization is when you create these images yourself. Guided imagery is when you listen to someone's voice guiding you on this mental journey.

To practice, simply close your eyes and create a vivid mental image of a place where you feel completely safe and relaxed. It could be the backwaters of Kerala, a peaceful temple, or a beautiful mountain view from your last holiday. Try to use all your senses. What do you see? What do you hear? What do you smell?

The science behind this is fascinating. Your brain often cannot tell the difference between a real experience and a vividly imagined one. When you imagine a peaceful scene, your body responds as if you are actually there. Your heart rate slows down, your muscles relax, and your body enters the relaxation response.

Visualization is also a powerful tool for building confidence. Before a big presentation or a difficult conversation, you can close your eyes and visualize yourself handling the situation calmly and successfully. This mental rehearsal can significantly reduce your anxiety and improve your performance.

Whenever I need a moment of calm, I close my eyes and picture myself sitting on a quiet hill near my home in Pune, watching the sunset. In my mind, I can feel the cool evening breeze and see the sky turn from orange to purple. This simple mental trip, even for a minute, brings a deep sense of peace. Your mind's eye is a powerful tool. Use it to find your calm.

Yoga for Stress Relief: Our Ancient Medicine

For us in India, yoga is not a new trend. It is a priceless inheritance, a gift from our ancestors. Yoga is not just about twisting your body into difficult postures, or *asanas*. The word "yoga" itself means "union"—the union of mind, body, and spirit.

Yoga is a moving meditation. It combines physical postures, breathing exercises (*pranayama*), and mindfulness to create a profound sense of balance and well-being. It is one of the most powerful ways to manage stress.

A friend of mine Pratik, recalls his own journey with yoga began during the most difficult time of his life—shoulder muscle tear. He recalls that the stress was so intense that his body felt like it was made of stone. His muscles were in constant, painful knots. He started yoga just to stretch my body, but I discovered something much deeper.

The physical relief was wonderful, yes. But it was the mental and emotional release that truly changed him. On the yoga mat, he learned to focus on his breath and be present in his body. This sense of being grounded and centered didn't just stay on the mat. It started to come with him into his daily life. It helped him navigate that professional difficult period with a newfound sense of balance.

You don't have to be flexible to start yoga. There are gentle, simple routines that anyone can do. A few rounds of the **Sun Salutation** (*Surya Namaskar*) in the morning can energize your whole day. A few gentle stretches before bed can help you sleep peacefully.

The breath is the heart of yoga. When you link your breath with your movement, the practice becomes a beautiful dance that calms your mind. With every deep inhale, you bring in energy and positivity. With every long exhale, you release tension and negativity.

You don't need a fancy studio. You just need a small space and a willingness to connect with yourself. Yoga is a journey back to your own inner peace. Roll out your mat, take a deep breath, and welcome this ancient wisdom into your life.

The Magic of Appreciation: Counting Your Blessings

Our minds have a strange habit. We can have a hundred good things happen in a day, and one bad thing. What do we focus on? The one bad thing. This is called the "negativity bias." It's an old survival mechanism. But in our modern lives, it can be a major source of stress.

An **appreciation or gratitude journal** is a simple but magical tool to change this habit. It is like a personal coach that trains your mind to see the good.

The practice is very simple. Every night before you sleep, take a notebook and write down three things that you are grateful for from your day. They don't have to be big things. It could be the taste of your morning *chai*, a kind word from a colleague, the laughter of your child, or the comfort of your bed. Also, write down one thing you appreciate about yourself.

This simple act, done consistently, can rewire your brain. It shifts your focus from what is wrong in your life to what is right. It builds a mindset of positivity and resilience. The benefits are not just about feeling happy. It builds your emotional strength and helps you handle stress with more grace.

The science on this is very clear. Practicing gratitude can change your brain activity, reduce symptoms of depression and anxiety, and improve your mood. It's like a natural medicine for your soul.

My girlfriend and I started a simple ritual years ago. We leave little sticky notes for each other with a small message of appreciation. "Thank you for making my favourite dinner." "I appreciate how hard you work for us." These small notes are little deposits of love and gratitude that have strengthened our relationship immensely.

Appreciation is not about ignoring the problems in your life. It is about choosing to also see the blessings. With every word of gratitude you write, you are not just filling a page. You are welcoming positivity that will bring warmth and light to your life.

CHAPTER SIX - The Art of Being Your Own Best Friend

Imagine your child comes home from school with a bad report card. They are upset and scared. What would you do? Would you scold them, call them a failure, and tell them they are no good?

Of course not. You would probably hug them. You would say, "It's okay. These things happen. Let's see how we can do better next time. I am with you."

Now, let me ask you another question. When you make a mistake, when you fail at something, when you are having a really hard day... what do you say to yourself?

Most of us have an inner voice, an "inner critic," that is very harsh. It scolds us, judges us, and tells us we are not good enough. We would never speak to a friend the way we often speak to ourselves.

Self-compassion is simply about changing this. It is about treating yourself with the same kindness, care, and understanding that you would offer to a friend you love. It is about giving yourself a mental hug when you are struggling and whispering to yourself, "It's okay. You are doing the best you can."

Self-compassion is not about making excuses or feeling sorry for yourself. It is about recognizing that life is hard, and being human means making mistakes. It means being patient with yourself as you learn and grow. It's like being your own best friend, one who is always there to offer a gentle pat on the back.

Dr.Deepak Chopra, a famous researcher, says that self-compassion has three main parts:

1. **Self-Kindness:** This means being warm and understanding towards yourself when you are suffering, instead of being cold and critical. Think of how a mother speaks to her child. That is self-kindness.
2. **Common Humanity:** This is the beautiful understanding that you are not alone in your struggles. Everyone in this world suffers. Everyone makes mistakes. Your pain is not a sign that something is wrong with you. It is a sign that you are a part of the human family. When we remember this, we feel less isolated.
3. **Mindfulness:** This means looking at your difficult thoughts and feelings with a balanced awareness. Not ignoring them, but also not getting lost in them. It is like watching a storm from inside a safe house. You see the rain and the wind, but you are not swept away by it.

When you practice self-compassion, it becomes a powerful shield against stress. It lowers anxiety and depression. It builds your emotional strength, allowing you to bounce back from problems more quickly. It’s like having a strong, flexible bamboo tree inside you that can bend in the wind but never breaks.

Self-compassion is different from self-esteem. Self-esteem is often about feeling good about your successes. But what happens when you fail? Your self-esteem can crash. Self-compassion, on the other hand, is always there for you. It is a steady source of strength that does not depend on whether you win or lose. It is a friend who holds your hand in good times and bad.

A Moment for You: Self-Compassion Exercise

Think about something that has been bothering you recently, a mistake you made or a challenge you are facing. Now, take a piece of paper and write a small note. But imagine you are writing it not to yourself, but to a very dear friend who is going through the same thing. What would you say to them? How would you offer them kindness and support? Read that note. Those are the words you deserve to hear.

Taming Your Inner Critic: Changing the Voice in Your Head

We all have it. That nagging voice in our head. The one that loves to point out our mistakes. The one that compares us to "*Sharma ji ka beta*" who is always doing better. The one that whispers, "You're not smart enough," "You're not successful enough," "You messed up again."

This inner voice, our "inner critic," can be our biggest source of stress. It can make a small mistake feel like a huge disaster. It’s like having a personal commentator in your head who only says negative things. Where does this voice come from? Often, it is the echo of our past—the voice of a strict teacher, a critical parent, or the pressures of society that tell us we must always be perfect.

But we do not have to be a slave to this voice. We can learn to transform it.

The first step is to simply notice it. When you hear that negative self-talk, just become aware of it. Try to see it as a separate character, not as the "truth." You can even give it a funny name. This helps you get some distance from it.

The next step is to question it. When your inner critic says, "You are a failure," ask it gently, "Is that really true? Or did I just make one mistake? Haven't I succeeded at many other things?"

This is a technique called **cognitive reframing**. It means changing the story you tell yourself. Instead of, "I am not good enough," you can reframe it to, "I am learning and growing. Every mistake is a lesson."

Another powerful practice is **loving-kindness meditation**. It is a simple meditation where you send kind and compassionate wishes to yourself. You sit quietly and repeat phrases like, "May I be happy. May I be healthy. May I be safe. May I live with ease." It is like watering a plant with love. Slowly, the harsh voice of the critic starts to become softer, and the voice of kindness starts to become stronger.

Let me tell you about Madhav, a young artist I know. He was very talented, but his inner critic was destroying his confidence. Every time he painted, the voice would tell him, "This is not good enough. No one will like it." He would get so stressed that he would stop painting.

He started a simple practice. Every time the critical voice appeared, he would stop, take a breath, and say to it, "Thank you for sharing, but I am the artist here." Then he would deliberately say something kind to himself, like, "I enjoy the process of painting." Over time, the critic lost its power. Madhav started to enjoy his art again, and his work became even more beautiful.

Remember, the goal is not to kill the inner critic. It is to transform it from a critic into a kind guide.

The Science of Self-Compassion: How Kindness Heals

Self-compassion may sound like a soft, emotional idea, but it has hard scientific proof behind it. Researchers have found that it has real, measurable benefits for our mind and body.

Studies show that people who practice self-compassion have lower levels of anxiety, stress, and depression. It acts like an emotional shock absorber, protecting you from the bumps and jolts of life. When you are kind to yourself, you become more resilient. You are able to handle setbacks and bounce back much faster.

The science goes even deeper. Self-compassion can actually change your brain. When you are being kind to yourself, you activate the parts of your brain that are associated with feelings of safety, comfort, and care. It's like your brain is getting a warm, soothing hug. This process reduces the activity in the "threat" part of your brain (the amygdala). So, you literally start to feel safer and less panicked in stressful situations.

And what about the body? The impact is profound. Self-compassion has been shown to lower the levels of **cortisol**, our main stress hormone. As we know, high cortisol is like a slow poison for our body. By being kind to ourselves, we create an inner environment where cortisol levels naturally go down. This reduces the physical damage of stress.

Self-compassion has also been linked to a higher **heart rate variability (HRV)**. As we discussed, HRV is a sign of a healthy, resilient heart and nervous system. A higher HRV means your body is better at adapting to stress. Self-compassion is like a workout for your heart's resilience.

Think of it this way: when you are hard on yourself, your body goes into a state of threat (fight-or-flight). When you are compassionate with yourself, your body goes into a state of safety and care (rest-and-digest). By choosing compassion, you are choosing health.

Self-Compassion at Work: A Secret to Success

The workplace can often feel like a high-pressure battlefield. Deadlines, targets, competition—it can be incredibly stressful. In this environment, self-compassion is not a weakness. It is a secret ingredient for strength and success.

When you manage your work stress with self-compassion, you can handle the pressure without burning out. You improve your job satisfaction and your performance. When you are kind to yourself after making a mistake, you are less likely to get stuck in fear and more likely to learn from it and move on.

How can you practice this at work?

- **Take Mindful Breaks:** Even just two minutes away from your desk can make a difference. Step away, stretch, and take a few deep breaths. It's like a mini-vacation for your brain.
- **Set Realistic Goals:** It is easy to fall into the trap of trying to do everything perfectly. This is a recipe for burnout. Set achievable goals. And remember, it's okay to say "no" sometimes.
- **Remember Common Humanity:** When you are having a tough day at work, remind yourself that you are not alone. Your colleagues, even your boss, have their own struggles and bad days. This thought can make you feel more connected and less stressed.

I'll never forget a story a young dentist, Radhika, shared in one of my workshops. She was doing a difficult root canal procedure and ran into a problem she couldn't solve. She had to stop and refer the patient to a specialist. She felt mortified, like a complete failure.

Her inner critic was screaming at her: *"You are so stupid! Your assistant thinks you are a loser. The patient will never trust you again."*

As she shared this story with the group, I saw heads nodding all around the room. When she finished, a fellow senior dentists spoke up. He told her, "Radhika, this has happened to all of us, more times than we can count. It is part of the job."

In that moment, Radhika felt a huge wave of relief. Her personal failure became a shared human experience. She was not alone. That is the power of common humanity.

When we are kinder to ourselves, we also become kinder and more understanding towards others. A compassionate work culture is a productive and happy one.

Emotional Intelligence: The Skill of Smart Emotions

Imagine you have a superpower. The power to understand your own feelings, and the feelings of others, and use that understanding to make better decisions. That superpower is called **Emotional Intelligence (EI)**.

It's like having an inner GPS that helps you navigate the complex world of human relationships. EI has a few key parts:

- **Self-Awareness:** Knowing what you are feeling and why.
- **Self-Regulation:** Managing your emotions, so they don't control you.
- **Empathy:** Understanding how others are feeling.

- **Social Skills:** Using this understanding to build strong relationships.

Improving your emotional intelligence is like tuning a musical instrument. It brings harmony to your life. You can start with simple exercises. For example, **active listening**. When someone is talking, don't just wait for your turn to speak. Really listen. Listen to their words, their tone of voice, their body language. Try to understand the feeling behind their words.

High EI is a powerful tool for stress management. When you understand your emotions, you can handle conflicts more calmly. An argument becomes a conversation, not a battle. Teamwork at your job becomes smoother because you can understand your colleagues' perspectives.

Take the story of James, a manager who was in a very high-stress job. His team was always tense and unhappy. He learned about emotional intelligence and started practicing empathy. He began to listen to his team's concerns without judgment. He started to understand their pressures. This one change transformed the atmosphere. The team became more supportive, their work improved, and James's own stress levels went down dramatically.

Emotional intelligence is your ally in life. It helps you build strong, healthy relationships at home and at work. It reduces stress by helping you navigate the emotional world with wisdom and grace. It’s not about being perfect. It is about being human, with a little more understanding and a lot more heart.

CHAPTER SEVEN - Weaving Peace into Your Busy Day: Simple Daily Habits

Imagine you are standing at a chaotic city intersection, like Mumbai's Dadar station during peak hour. The noise of the local trains, the shouts of the vendors, the sheer number of people—it's overwhelming. But what if I told you that you could find a moment of complete peace, right there in the middle of all that chaos?

That is the power of **micro-meditations**. These are very short, bite-sized moments of mindfulness that you can practice anywhere, anytime. They can be as short as 10 seconds or as long as a few minutes. They are like small pause buttons you can press during a busy day to reset your mind and calm your nerves.

Picture this: you are waiting for the lift in your office building. Instead of impatiently checking your phone, you take one deep breath. Inhale slowly, exhale slowly. That's it. You just did a micro-meditation. You are standing in a queue at the grocery store. Instead of getting frustrated, you focus on the feeling of your feet on the floor for a few seconds. That is a micro-meditation.

These tiny practices are incredibly efficient. They give you immediate stress relief without needing a lot of time. They sharpen your focus, like a mental cup of coffee without the jitters. By weaving these small moments of mindfulness into your daily activities, you build a powerful buffer against stress.

Let me tell you about Dr. Haldar, an emergency room doctor in a busy hospital in Kolkata. The stress and chaos of his job were relentless. He started practicing micro-meditations. While washing his hands between patients, he would take three conscious breaths. While walking down the long hospital corridor, he would focus on the sensation of his footsteps. These tiny islands of calm in his sea of chaos became his lifeline. They helped him stay centered and make clear decisions even in the most high-pressure situations.

A Moment for You: Quick Breathing Exercise

Try this right now. Close your eyes. Take a deep breath in through your nose for a count of four. Hold it for a count of four. Now, exhale slowly through your mouth for a count of six. Repeat this just three times. Notice how you feel. A little calmer? A little more centered? That's the magic.

Micro-meditations remind us that peace is not something we have to go searching for on a distant mountain top. It is a state of mind we can create, one mindful breath at a time, right here in the middle of our busy lives.

Digital Detox: Disconnecting to Reconnect with Yourself

Think of your brain as a computer that has too many tabs open at once: WhatsApp, Instagram, email, news alerts. Each one is beeping and demanding your attention. After a while, the computer starts to slow down and hang. Imagine having all those tabs open in your browser, you will never be able to focus, even if you could, it would be at the pace of a snail. No, that's not your old age catching up to you if that is your excuse, you need to close those tabs!

A **digital detox** is simply your chance to close some of those tabs. It is about taking a conscious break from the screens that have become our constant companions. In our hyper-connected world, a digital detox is like taking a deep, clean breath of fresh air after being in a stuffy room. It is essential for restoring our ability to focus.

How can you do a digital detox without feeling like you are cut off from the world? Start small.

- **Create Tech-Free Times:** Make mealtimes a no-phone zone. Use this time to actually talk to your family.
- **Create Tech-Free Zones:** Make your bedroom a screen-free sanctuary. This will dramatically improve your sleep. Don't check your phone first thing in the morning or last thing at night.
- **Set a Digital Curfew:** Decide on a time in the evening, say 9 PM, after which all screens are off.

The benefits are huge. You will sleep better. Your mind will feel less cluttered and more focused. And most importantly, you will have more time and attention for real, face-to-face interactions with the people you love.

Let me share a story. Few years ago, when I went to Jammu and Kashmir. There was no mobile network for my prepaid sim card. The first day was difficult. I felt a constant urge to check my phone, to post a picture of the stunning mountains.

But from the second day, something shifted. Without the distraction of my phone, I started to notice everything more deeply. The colours of the mountains, the sound of the wind, the taste of the simple food. I had real conversations with my friend who was with me. By the end of the trip, I felt a sense of peace and clarity that I hadn't felt in years. It was a powerful reminder that the best connections are not online.

A digital detox is not about hating technology. It is about using it consciously, so that it serves you, and you don't become its slave.

Sleep Hygiene: The Foundation of Good Health

Imagine waking up in the morning feeling fresh, rested, and full of energy, ready to take on the day. That is the gift of a good night's sleep. **Sleep hygiene** is simply the collection of good habits that help you get that gift every night.

Sleep is not a luxury; it is a biological necessity. It is your body's nightly repair and maintenance cycle. When you sleep, your body balances its stress hormones, like cortisol. A good night's sleep is one of the most powerful stress-busters available. When you are well-rested, your mood is better, your mind is sharper, and you are better able to handle challenges.

How can you improve your sleep hygiene?

- **Have a Fixed Schedule:** Try to go to bed and wake up at roughly the same time every day, even on weekends. This sets your body's internal clock, or *biorhythm*.
- **Create a Restful Environment:** Your bedroom should be for sleeping. Keep it dark, quiet, and cool. As we discussed, banish screens from the bedroom.
- **Have a Wind-Down Routine:** In the hour before bed, do calming activities. Read a book (a real one, not on a screen!), listen to soft music, or take a warm bath. This signals to your brain that it's time to switch off.

Lack of sleep, on the other hand, is a recipe for disaster. It makes you irritable and emotional. It clouds your judgment. It creates a vicious cycle: stress makes it hard to sleep, and lack of sleep makes you more stressed.

Sleep is not wasted time. It is a non-negotiable part of a healthy, stress-free life. Prioritize it as you would an important meeting.

Physical Activity: Moving Your Body to Calm Your Mind

For me, exercise is non-negotiable. You don't have to love it. **You just have to do it!**

When you exercise, your body releases wonderful chemicals called **endorphins**. These are our body's natural happiness pills. They lift your mood and give you that positive feeling, often called a "runner's high."

But that's not all. Regular exercise also reduces the levels of stress hormones like cortisol. It's like a daily cleaning service for the stress in your body.

You don't need a fancy gym membership. The key is to find a form of movement that you can do consistently.

- **Walking:** A brisk 30-minute walk every day is one of the best forms of exercise.
- **Yoga:** As we discussed, it's a wonderful way to build both physical and mental strength.
- **Dancing:** Put on your favourite music and just move!
- **Playing a Sport:** A game of cricket or badminton with friends is a great way to exercise and connect with others.

The impact of exercise on mental health is incredible. It is one of the most effective natural anti-anxiety and anti-depressant treatments. It also boosts your self-esteem and confidence. As you see your body getting stronger, you start to feel mentally stronger too.

Physical activity is a powerful promise you make to yourself for a healthier body and a calmer mind. Lace up your shoes and take that first step, and you'll immediately start feeling at least 5 years younger.

Nutrition and Stress: You Are What You Eat

Your body is like a temple. And the food you eat is the offering you make to it. The connection between what you eat and how you feel is very deep.

Our traditional Indian wisdom has always known this. The food we eat can be *sattvic* (pure and calming), *rajasic* (stimulating), or *tamasic* (dulling). Modern nutrition science confirms this. The food you eat directly affects your brain chemistry and your mood. A diet full of processed junk food, sugar, and unhealthy fats is like fuel for stress and anxiety. A diet rich in fresh fruits, vegetables, whole grains, and healthy proteins is like a calming balm for your mind.

The **Mediterranean diet**, which is very similar to a traditional, balanced Indian diet, is excellent for managing stress. It's rich in all the good things that nourish your brain. The key is to focus on fresh, home-cooked food (*ghar ka khana*).

Also, be mindful of your blood sugar. When you eat a lot of sugar or refined flour (*maida*), your blood sugar shoots up and then crashes, leaving you feeling tired and irritable. Eating balanced meals with protein and fibre keeps your blood sugar stable, which keeps your mood stable too.

Stress can often make us **emotional eaters**. After a hard day, we reach for that packet of chips or that box of sweets for comfort. The first step is to become aware of this pattern. When you feel the urge to eat, ask yourself: "Am I really hungry, or am I feeling stressed, bored, or sad?"

Practicing **mindful eating** can help. Eat slowly. Savour each bite. Pay attention to the colours, smells, and tastes of your food. This not only helps with digestion but also builds a healthier relationship with food.

Remember, food is not just fuel. It is medicine. By making conscious, healthy choices, you are nourishing your body and your mind, and building a strong foundation for a life with less stress.

CHAPTER EIGHT - Finding Your Own Path: Creating a Plan for Your Life

Imagine you go to a tailor to get a shirt stitched. The tailor doesn't just give you a shirt off the rack. They take your measurements. They ask you what style you want. They create a shirt that is a perfect fit for you.

A stress management plan should be like that tailor-made shirt. It should be designed specifically for you. A one-size-fits-all approach doesn't work, because your life, your stressors, and your personality are unique.

The first step in creating your plan is **self-assessment**. Before you can solve a problem, you have to understand it. You have to become a detective in your own life.

What are your personal stressors?

- **External Stressors:** These are the things happening outside of you. A difficult boss, a long commute in traffic, financial pressures, family responsibilities.
- **Internal Stressors:** These are the things happening inside you. The habit of perfectionism, negative self-talk, the fear of failure, the need to please everyone.

One simple exercise I love is the **"Energy Battery."** Take a piece of paper. On one side, list all the things in your day that drain your energy and make you feel stressed. On the other side, list all the things that charge your battery and make you feel good. This simple map can give you amazing clarity about where your stress is coming from and what you can do to feel better.

Setting Your Intentions: Your Personal Roadmap

Once you know your stressors, the next step is to set clear goals for how you want to manage them. Trying to reduce stress without clear goals is like trying to travel to a new city without a map. You will just wander around and get lost.

This is where **SMART goals** come in. SMART stands for:

- **S**pecific: Be very clear. Not "I want to be less stressed," but "I will practice 10 minutes of breathing exercises every morning."
- **M**easurable: How will you know you have achieved it? "I will do it five days a week."
- **A**chievable: Is your goal realistic? Don't try to change everything at once. Start small.
- **R**elevant: Is this goal important to you? Does it align with your values?

- Time-bound: Give yourself a deadline. "I will do this for the next four weeks and then see how I feel."

Breaking down a big goal into small, manageable steps is the key to success. For example, if your big goal is to improve your health, a small SMART goal could be: "I will go for a 20-minute walk after dinner, three times this week."

Setting clear goals gives you a sense of control and empowerment. Every time you achieve a small goal, it motivates you to keep going.

Crafting Your Daily Routine: A Framework for Calm

A structured daily routine is like the foundation of a strong building. It gives your life stability and predictability, which reduces anxiety. Our ancient Ayurvedic tradition talks about the importance of *dinacharya*—a daily routine that is in harmony with the rhythms of nature. Its okay if you cannot be in-line with the nature, but having a routine is a must!

When you have a consistent time for waking up, eating your meals, and sleeping, your body and mind feel safe and balanced.

Incorporating stress relief into your daily routine is the best way to make it a habit.

- **Morning Ritual:** Start your day with a few minutes of calm, before the chaos begins. It could be meditation, a few yoga stretches, or simply sipping your *chai* in silence.
- **Evening Ritual:** Create a routine to wind down at night. Turn off screens, listen to soft music, read a book. This tells your body it's time to prepare for sleep.

A good routine doesn't have to be rigid. Think of it as a flexible framework, not a prison. It reduces the number of small decisions you have to make every day, freeing up your mental energy for more important things.

Adapting Techniques: Finding Your Perfect Fit

Stress management is like a buffet. There are many different dishes on offer—meditation, yoga, exercise, journaling, and so on. Your job is to try a little bit of everything and see what you like best.

Personalization is crucial. What works wonders for your friend might not work for you. Be open to experimenting. Try a new technique for a week and see how it feels. Does it make you feel calmer? Is it easy to fit into your life?

For me, cooking is a form of meditation. The simple act of creating something, the sound of spices sizzling in hot oil—it brings me into the present moment and calms my mind. I learned this when I started living alone, so I had to be creative with whatever ingredients I had. That resourcefulness, which is so common in Indian kitchens, is a powerful stress-buster.

For you, it might be painting, gardening, singing, or playing a musical instrument. The key is to find activities that help you get into a state of "flow," where you are so absorbed in what you are doing that you forget your worries.

Your stress management plan is a living thing. It will change as you change. Be flexible. Keep learning. The journey of stress management is a journey of self-discovery.

Building Your Support Network: The Power of We

In India, we have a beautiful saying: *"Akela chana bhad nahi phod sakta."* One person alone cannot achieve great things. This is especially true when it comes to managing stress. We are not meant to face life's challenges alone.

Your **support network**—your family, your friends, your community—is one of your most precious assets. Social support is the emotional cushion that protects you from the hard falls of life. It is the feeling of knowing that there are people who care about you, who will listen to you without judgment, and who will be there for you no matter what.

Building and nurturing this network is essential.

- **Connect with Family:** Make time for the people who matter most.
- **Nurture Friendships:** Call that old college friend you haven't spoken to in ages. Meet your friends for a cup of coffee.
- **Find Your Tribe:** Join a group or a class where you can meet people with similar interests.

A strong support system reduces feelings of loneliness and isolation, which are major triggers for stress and depression. It gives you a sense of belonging.

I still have fond memories from my college days. After a stressful week of exams, my friends and I would gather at our favourite *dhaba.* We would share stories of our struggles and our small victories. We would laugh at our mistakes until our stomachs hurt. In those moments of shared laughter and connection, the stress of the week would just melt away. We were there for each other. That camaraderie gave us the strength to face the next challenge.

Tracking Your Progress: Celebrating Your Journey

Imagine you are on a long journey by train. Looking out the window and seeing the stations pass by gives you a sense of progress, a feeling that you are moving forward.

Tracking your progress in your stress management journey does the same thing. It keeps you motivated and helps you see how far you have come.

How can you track your progress?

- **Journaling:** A stress management journal is a wonderful tool. You can write about your challenges, your successes, and what you are learning.
- **Mood Tracking Apps:** There are many simple apps that can help you track your mood and stress levels.

- **Regular Reflection:** Once a week, take 10 minutes to think about your journey. What worked well this week? What was challenging? What can you do differently next week?

Reflection helps you celebrate your small wins. It helps you learn from your setbacks. It helps you adapt your plan as you go along.

Remember, creating a personal stress management plan is not another stressful task to add to your to-do list. It is an act of self-love. It is a commitment you make to yourself for a healthier, happier, and more peaceful life.

CHAPTER NINE - "But I Have No Time..." and Other Truths About Stress

Imagine you are trying to fit a large, square box into a small, round suitcase. That's what managing stress can sometimes feel like. You have your work deadlines, your family responsibilities, your child's school project, and a hundred other things. Life gives you a to-do list that is longer than a train, and every task feels like you are trying to balance another spinning plate on a stick.

For most of us, the problem is not that we don't *want* to reduce our stress. The problem is finding the time and energy to do it. You might think, "Stress management? Yes, that sounds lovely. I will schedule it for next month, right after I solve all the other problems in the universe."

But before you give up and surrender to the chaos, let's talk about how small, simple habits—like little drops of water—can fill a big pot of peace over time.

"I Have No Time!": Stress Relief for a Busy Life

Let's be honest. Modern Indian life can feel like a race against the clock. The work pressure is immense, the traffic is a nightmare, and our family and social duties are endless. Between a demanding job, taking care of children and parents, and attending family functions, finding time for ourselves can feel like a distant dream.

So, stress relief often gets pushed to the bottom of our priority list. But ignoring stress is like ignoring a leaky tap. It doesn't stop on its own. It just keeps dripping, and one day you wake up to a flooded room.

But what if I told you that finding time for stress relief is not about adding another big task to your list? It is about weaving small, peaceful moments into the day you already have.

This is the magic of **micro-habits**. These are tiny, manageable actions that you can do in just a minute or two. Think of them as small, hidden treasures of calm in your busy day.

- **Mindful Moments:** While you are waiting for your *chai* to boil, just stand and take three deep breaths.
- **While Commuting:** If you are stuck in traffic, instead of getting angry, use that time. Listen to some calming music. Or just notice your breath. It can transform a stressful commute into a few moments of peace.
- **At Your Desk:** Every hour, just stand up, stretch your arms, and look out the window for one minute. This small break can refresh your mind more than you can imagine.

Small changes, like scheduling a five-minute break in your calendar, can have a huge impact. Consider Rajini, an entrepreneur in Bangalore who felt like she was drowning in work. She started "time blocking." She would schedule her entire day, including short 10-minute breaks for a quick walk or some deep breathing. This simple habit gave her a sense of control and dramatically reduced her stress.

Or think of Sameer, a busy father in Delhi. He started waking up just 15 minutes before the rest of his family. He used that quiet time to sit in his balcony with a cup of tea and just be with himself. Those 15 minutes of peace changed the tone of his entire day.

You don't need to find an extra hour. Just find the small moments that are already there. Reclaim them for yourself. One small, peaceful moment at a time.

"Is This All Mumbo-Jumbo?": Understanding the Science

I understand. When you first hear words like "mindfulness" or "meditation," you might picture a sadhu in the Himalayas. It can sound a bit like mystical, unscientific *"hocus pocus."*

It's normal to be skeptical. Does focusing on your breath really do anything? Is this just a new trend?

The good news is that these practices are not based on wishful thinking. Our ancient Indian traditions of Yoga and Ayurveda have known about the power of the mind for thousands of years. And now, modern science is proving this ancient wisdom with hard data.

As we've discussed, scientists can now use advanced machines to see what happens inside the brain during meditation. And what they have found is amazing. Regular meditation can physically change your brain. It strengthens the areas responsible for focus, emotional control, and compassion. It's like taking your brain to the gym.

How do these practices work? They activate your body's "rest and digest" system—the natural off-switch for stress. This lowers the levels of stress hormones like cortisol. It's not just about "feeling" calm. Your body is actually becoming calmer at a biological level. These practices are about learning to manage your own nervous system, which gives you more control over your life and your health.

Today, many doctors and healthcare professionals are recommending these techniques to their patients. Take my friend, Dr. Gupta, a cardiologist. He tells all his heart patients to practice simple breathing exercises. He says, "I can give you medicine for your heart, but you have the power to give your heart peace."

So, if you have been skeptical, I invite you to just try. You don't have to believe in anything. Just do the practice for a few weeks and see how you feel. Your own experience will be the greatest proof.

"I'm Afraid to Show My Weakness": The Courage to Be Vulnerable

Imagine you are invited to speak on a stage. The thought of showing your deepest feelings, your fears, and your struggles in front of others can feel terrifying. It can feel like standing emotionally naked in a crowded room.

This is the fear of **vulnerability**. In our society, especially for men, we are often taught that showing our emotions is a sign of weakness. We are told to be strong, to "man up," to keep our problems to ourselves.

So, when it comes to stress, we often wear a mask. We pretend everything is fine, even when we are crumbling on the inside. We are afraid that if we admit we are struggling, people will judge us or think less of us.

But here is the truth: **Vulnerability is not weakness. It is courage.** It is the courage to be real, to be human. And it is the only path to true healing and connection.

When we share our struggles in a safe space—with a trusted friend, a family member, or in a support group—something magical happens. The burden on our heart becomes lighter. And we often discover that we are not alone. Others are carrying similar burdens. That feeling of shared humanity is incredibly healing.

Let me tell you about a powerful moment in one of my workshops. We were doing an exercise where people share a stressful experience. At first, everyone was hesitant. But then, one man, a senior manager in a big company, started talking about the immense pressure he was under and how he felt like a failure. His voice was shaking.

When he finished, there was a moment of silence. And then, another person started sharing, and then another. A wave of connection and understanding filled the room. The masks came off. In that moment of shared vulnerability, they found not weakness, but incredible strength and unity.

If you are afraid to open up, start small. Find one person you trust completely. Or consider talking to a professional counsellor. Remember to practice self-compassion. Be as kind to yourself as you would be to a friend.

My own journey with this was not easy. Growing up, emotions were not something we talked about. The idea of crying felt like a monumental failure. But during the most difficult time of my life, I learned that my tears were not a sign of weakness, but a sign of my heart's ability to heal.

Embracing vulnerability is not about losing control. It is about gaining freedom. The freedom to be your authentic self.

"I Must Be Perfect": Letting Go of Perfectionism

Do you ever feel like you are running in a never-ending race to be perfect? The perfect employee, the perfect parent, the perfect spouse, the perfect child.

Perfectionism is a very heavy burden to carry. It is the belief that anything less than flawless is a failure. It whispers in your ear that you must always do more, be more, and achieve more. While wanting to do your best is a good thing, perfectionism turns this desire into a source of constant stress and anxiety. The fear of making a mistake can be so paralyzing that you stop trying new things. *I have myself been a victim of perfectionism, still am, but I have now learnt to manage myself effectively. By following the principles I have told you, so can you!*

The first step is to shift your mindset from **perfection** to **progress**. Imagine you are climbing a mountain. Perfectionism tells you that the only thing that matters is reaching the summit. It ignores the entire journey. A progress-oriented mindset, on the other hand, celebrates every step you take. It understands that there will be slips and falls, but each one is a lesson.

Celebrate your small victories. Did you complete a difficult task at work? Acknowledge it. Did you manage to stay calm in a stressful situation? Pat yourself on the back.

Setting realistic goals is key. Remember the SMART goals we talked about. They help you break down a big, intimidating goal into small, achievable steps. And practice gratitude. Be thankful for what you have achieved, instead of always focusing on what you haven't.

Consider Barbara, an artist who was so afraid of not painting a "perfect" masterpiece that she stopped painting altogether. Her creativity was frozen by fear. When she learned to embrace a progress mindset, she started to enjoy the process of painting again. She allowed herself to make "mistakes." And ironically, her work became more beautiful and authentic than ever before.

Choosing progress over perfection is a radical act of self-kindness. It is about giving yourself permission to be human. Remember, life is not a performance to be perfected. It is a journey to be lived.

CHAPTER TEN - Finding Your 'Why': The Path to Lasting Peace

Imagine your brain is like a city with many roads. When you have a habit, like getting stressed in traffic, it's like a big, wide highway in your brain. Your thoughts automatically travel down this road.

Neuroplasticity is the amazing, scientific truth that you can build new roads in your brain. Your brain is not fixed like a stone. It is flexible, like plasticine. It can change and reorganize itself based on your experiences and practices. Every time you choose to respond to traffic with a deep breath instead of anger, you are laying the first stones of a new, calmer road in your brain.

Meditation and mindfulness are like the expert road-builders for your brain. With consistent practice, you can make the "calm" roads wider and smoother, and the old "stress" highways narrower and less used. It’s like upgrading your brain’s entire traffic system.

But it’s not just meditation. **Learning new things** is also a powerful way to keep your brain healthy and flexible. It’s like adding new, interesting destinations to your city map. Learning a new language, a musical instrument, or even a new recipe stimulates your brain and builds its resilience.

A Moment for You: Reflection Exercise

Think of something new you would love to learn. It doesn't have to be big or complicated. Maybe you want to learn how to cook a new dish, or learn a few words in a new language, or learn how to use a new app on your phone. Write it down. Taking that first small step to learn something new is a wonderful gift to your brain.

I have seen this in my own life. To share these ideas with more people, I had to learn about things I never thought I would—computers, marketing, website design. It was challenging, but also exciting. It showed me that we are never too old to learn and grow. Your brain is a dynamic, ever-changing marvel. Embrace its power to change, and you can change your life.

Embracing Change: The Art of Flowing with the River

Life is like a river. It is always flowing, always changing. Sometimes the current is gentle, sometimes it is fast and turbulent. We cannot stop the river from flowing. But we can learn to become better boatmen.

Embracing change is a crucial skill for a happy life. Resisting change is like trying to row your boat against the current. It is exhausting and futile. Learning to go with the flow, to adapt, is the secret to navigating life's transitions with grace.

How can we do this?

- **Don't Get Attached to the Outcome:** In the Bhagavad Gita, Lord Krishna teaches Arjun to focus on his *dharma* (duty) without being attached to the fruits of his actions. This is a profound lesson in managing change. Do your best, but let go of the need to control everything.
- **Set Realistic Expectations:** Acknowledge that change can be difficult. It's okay to feel sad about what is lost, while also being open to what is new.
- **Have a Proactive Mindset:** See change not as a threat, but as an opportunity. A job loss can be a chance to find a more fulfilling career. A move to a new city can be an exciting adventure.

Consider the story of Veerbhadra, who lost his corporate job during the pandemic. It was a huge shock. But instead of getting stuck in despair, he saw it as a sign. He had always loved carpentry. He used his time to learn more, and started a small business making beautiful wooden furniture from his home. The change he feared the most became the turning point that led him to a happier, more purposeful life.

Change is the only constant. When we learn to dance with it, instead of fighting it, life becomes a much more joyful journey.

The Art of Letting Go: Emptying Your Backpack

Imagine you are on a long trek, and you are carrying a heavy backpack. In this backpack, you are carrying rocks. Each rock has a name: an old grudge, a past hurt, a resentment you have been holding onto for years.

The trek is already difficult. But this heavy backpack is making it a thousand times harder.

Letting go of emotional baggage is like deciding to empty that backpack. Forgiveness is not a gift you give to the other person. It is a gift of freedom you give to yourself. Holding onto anger and resentment is like drinking poison and expecting the other person to die.

How can you start to let go?

- **Visualization:** Close your eyes. Imagine putting that heavy rock of resentment into a hot air balloon. Watch as the balloon slowly floats up into the sky and disappears. Feel the lightness in your heart.
- **Writing:** Write a letter to the person who hurt you. Pour out all your feelings on the paper. You don't have to send the letter. The act of writing itself is a powerful release. Then you can safely burn the letter, symbolizing that you are letting go.
- **Acceptance:** This is the most powerful tool. Sometimes, we have to accept that we cannot change the past. Wishing for a better past steals the peace from our present. Acceptance is about making peace with reality, so that you can move forward.

Many years ago, I lent a large sum of money to a very close friend. I did it out of love and trust. But as time went on, the friend started to avoid me, and the money was never returned. I felt so foolish and betrayed. The resentment I carried was like a constant, bitter taste in my mouth.

I finally realized that this anger was hurting me much more than it was hurting him. I had to let it go, for my own peace. It was not easy. I used visualization and compassion meditation. It didn't happen overnight. But slowly, I found myself reclaiming my inner peace. Letting go was not about him. It was about choosing freedom for myself.

Continuous Learning: Keeping Your Mind Alive

Your mind is like a garden. If you don't cultivate it, weeds will grow. **Lifelong learning** is the act of constantly planting new seeds of knowledge and curiosity in your mind.

Learning keeps your mind engaged, stimulated, and resilient. It gives you a sense of purpose and accomplishment. You can learn in many ways: read books, take an online course, attend workshops, or simply have conversations with people who know more than you.

Learning new skills also boosts your confidence. When you learn to do something new, whether it's cooking a new dish or using a new software, you prove to yourself that you are capable and adaptable.

Find what you are passionate about and learn more about it. My true passion is helping people live healthier lives. Even on my days off, I spend hours reading and learning about wellness. It doesn't feel like work. It feels like joy.

Celebrating Your Success: Acknowledging Your Journey

Imagine you have just finished cooking a special meal for your family. After everyone has eaten, you just quietly clean up. Wouldn't it feel better if someone said, "That was a delicious meal! Thank you!"?

We need to learn to say that to ourselves. **Celebrating your success**, no matter how small, is incredibly important. It reinforces your efforts and motivates you to keep going.

How can you celebrate?

- **Keep a Success Journal:** Every day, write down one thing you did well.
- **Share Your Victories:** Tell a friend or family member about a small win.
- **Treat Yourself:** Reward yourself with something small and enjoyable—a good book, a walk in the park, your favourite music.

When I was younger, I used to run for athletics. The training was gruelling. But I only ever thought about the finish line. I never stopped to appreciate the daily courage and determination it took just to train. Now, I look back and I wish I had celebrated those small victories along the way. Today, I take pride in the small things, like waking up early for a 20-minute workout.

Acknowledge your achievements with the joy they deserve. You have earned it.

Finding Your "Why": The Power of Purpose

Imagine two people are building a wall. You ask the first person, "What are you doing?" He says, "I am laying bricks." You ask the second person the same question. He looks up, with a light in his eyes, and says, "I am building a temple."

Who do you think has more motivation and resilience?

Having a clear sense of **purpose**—your "why"—is the ultimate buffer against stress. It is the North Star that guides you through difficult times. When you know *why* you are doing something, the *how* becomes easier.

I always ask people in my workshops: “Why did you choose your career?” Most people have a story, a deep emotional reason. I became a writer because I wanted to help people understand themselves and their world better. Remembering this "why" helps me push through the difficult days. It gives meaning to my struggles.

What is your "why"? Take some time to think about it. What are your values? What brings you a sense of meaning and fulfillment? Your purpose doesn't have to be grand. It can be simple: to be a good parent, to create beauty in the world, to help others.

When you are connected to your purpose, stress doesn't disappear. But it changes its meaning. It becomes a part of your journey, a challenge that helps you grow in service of something you believe in.

From Science to Practice: Living Your Stress Solution Every Day

My friend, we have come to the end of our journey together in this book. We have explored the science of stress and discovered a treasure chest of mind-body tools. We have learned that stress does not have to be the villain of our story.

We've learned that we have a built-in "off-switch"—the relaxation response. We've rediscovered the ancient wisdom of mindfulness, breathing, and yoga. We've learned the power of being kind to ourselves, of building connections, and of living with purpose.

But this book is not meant to be just read and kept on a shelf. It is meant to be lived. I encourage you to keep exploring, to keep practicing. Integrate these small habits into your daily life. Small steps, taken consistently, lead to big changes.

Stress is a part of life. But it does not have to define your life. You have the power to choose how you respond. You have the power to cultivate calm and resilience. And you are not alone on this journey.

Thank you for allowing me to be your guide. Now go forth and live your life with a calm mind, a strong spirit, and a heart full of joy. The world needs your unique light.

With gratitude and best wishes,

Atharva Inamdar

www.ingramcontent.com/pod-product-compliance
Ingram Content Group UK Ltd.
Pitfield, Milton Keynes, MK11 3LW, UK
UKHW021410190726
13845UKWH00028B/1007

9 789371 846509